Journey Along a River

The Nile

Jen Green

WAYLAND

This book is a differentiated text version of *A River Journey The Nile* by Rob Bowden.

This edition first published in 2009 by Wayland
Copyright © 2009 Wayland

Reprinted in 2010 by Wayland

Wayland
338 Euston Road
London NW1 3BH

Wayland
Level 17/207 Kent Street
Sydney NSW 2000

Editor: Victoria Brooker
Designer: Stephen Prosser

British Cataloguing in Publication Data
 Green, Jen.
  The Nile. -- (Journey along a river)
  1. Nile River--Juvenile literature. 2. Nile River Valley--
 Juvenile literature.
  I. Title II. Series
  916.2-dc22

ISBN: 978 0 7502 5869 2

Printed in China

Wayland is a division of Hachette Children's Books,
an Hachette UK company.
www.hachette.co.uk

Picture Acknowledgements

Cover © Robert Harding/Robert Harding World Imagery/Corbis; 1 Wayland Picture Library; 2, 5 Rob Bowden; 6 Andes Press Agency/Carlos Reyes-Manzo; 7 Bridgeman Art Library/Royal Geographical Society, London,UK; 8 T de Salis/Still Pictures; 9 (left) Caroline Penn/Impact; 9 (right), 10, 11 Rob Bowden; 12 Mark Deeble & Victoria Stone/Oxford Scientific Films; 13 (top) Joan Root/Oxford Scientific Films, (bottom) Fred Hoogervorst/Panos Pictures; 14 Richard Kemp/SAL/Oxford Scientific Films; 15 Robert Harding Picture Library; 16 (top) Art Wolfe/Science Photo Library; (bottom) G.Verhaegen/Still Pictures; 17 (top) Katri Burri/Panos Pictures, (bottom) Robert Harding Picture Library; 18 Trip/H Rogers; 19 Paul Almasy/Corbis; 20 Travel Ink/David Forman; 21 Topham; 22 NASA/Science Photo Library; 23 (top) Hutchison Picture Library, (bottom left) Trip/H Rogers, (bottom right) Impact?; 24 Colin Jones/Impact; 25, 26 Colin Jones/Impact; 27 (top) Toby Adamson/Still Pictures, (bottom) Eyal Bartov/Oxford Scientific Films; 28 Rob Bowden; 29 (top) Popperfoto, (bottom) Alex Dufort/Impact, (bottom right) Toby Adamson/Still Pictures); 30 Eye Ubiquitous/Julia Waterlow; 31 Peter Kingsford/Eye Ubiquitous; 32 (inset) Rob Bowden, (bottom) and 33 Peter Kingsford/Eye Ubiquitous; 34, 35, 36 Julia Waterlow/Eye Ubiquitous; 37 (top) David Keith Jones/Images of Africa, (bottom) Bojan Brecelj/Corbis; 38 Rob Bowden; 39 (top) Ecoscene/Mark Carey, (bottom) Impact; 40 Earth Satellite Corporation/Science Photo Library; 41 (top) Julia Waterlow/Eye Ubiquitous, (bottom) Bojan Brecelj/Still Pictures; 42 Hodder Wayland Picture Library; 43 Eye Ubiquitous/Steve Lindridge; 44 Gary John Norman/Panos Pictures

The maps in this book use a conical projection, and so the
indicator for North on the main map is only approximate.

Contents

Words in **bold** can be found in the glossary on page 47.

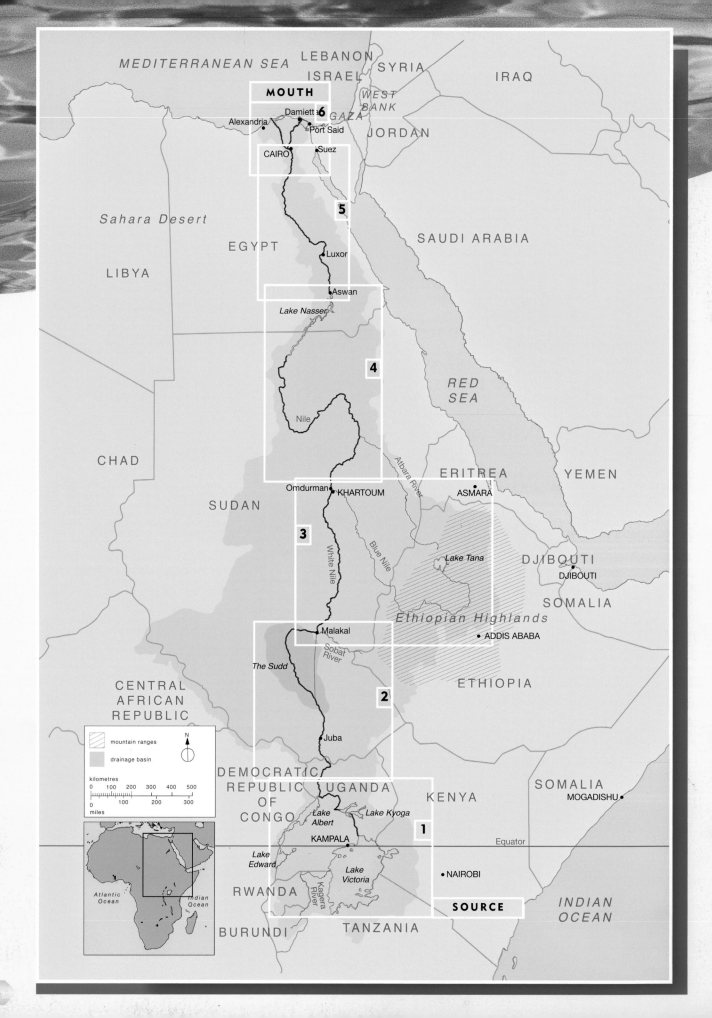

MEDITERRANEAN SEA

LEBANON
ISRAEL
SYRIA
IRAQ

WEST
BANK
GAZA
JORDAN

MOUTH

Alexandria
Damietta **6**
Port Said

CAIRO
Suez

Sahara Desert

EGYPT

5

LIBYA

Luxor

Aswan

Lake Nasser

SAUDI ARABIA

RED
SEA

YEMEN

4

Nile

CHAD

SUDAN

Atbara River

ERITREA

ASMARA

Omdurman KHARTOUM

3

White Nile

Blue Nile

Lake Tana

DJIBOUTI

DJIBOUTI

SOMALIA

Ethiopian Highlands

ADDIS ABABA

CENTRAL
AFRICAN
REPUBLIC

Malakal

Sobat
River

ETHIOPIA

The Sudd

2

Juba

mountain ranges

N

drainage basin

DEMOCRATIC
REPUBLIC
OF
CONGO

UGANDA

SOMALIA

kilometres
0   100   200   300   400   500

0   100   200   300
miles

Lake
Albert

KAMPALA

Lake Kyoga

KENYA

1

MOGADISHU

Equator

Atlantic
Ocean

Indian
Ocean

Lake
Edward

Kagera
River

Lake
Victoria

NAIROBI

RWANDA

SOURCE

INDIAN
OCEAN

BURUNDI

TANZANIA

4

Your guide to the river

Text themes

The Nile is the world's longest river, 6,670 kilometres long. It begins at Lake Victoria, Africa's biggest lake where three countries, Kenya, Tanzania and Uganda, meet. It then flows through swamps, over waterfalls and past cities before reaching the sea. The map on page 4 shows the whole length of the Nile River. The white squares show how our journey along the river has been divided into six chapters.

Map references

Each chapter has a map that shows the part of the river we are visiting. The numbered boxes show where interesting places are found.

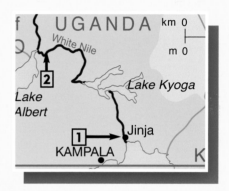

The journey ahead

Our journey starts where the White Nile leaves Lake Victoria, a huge lake in East Africa. It tumbles over waterfalls and then enters an enormous swamp called the Sudd.

Near the city of Khartoum the Blue Nile joins the White Nile. Now a single river, the Nile heads north into Egypt, where it has been dammed to create a huge lake called Lake Nasser. Beyond the dam the river flows through a barren desert. In Egypt we sail past temples and the famous pyramids to reach Cairo, one of Africa's biggest cities.

North of Cairo the river spreads out to make a huge, fan-shaped delta. Then it meets the Mediterranean Sea, at the end of its incredible 6,670 kilometre journey. As we travel the Nile we learn about the amazing places and people along its banks.

We board a small boat called a dhow to begin our journey. We sail on Lake Victoria to the source of the Nile.

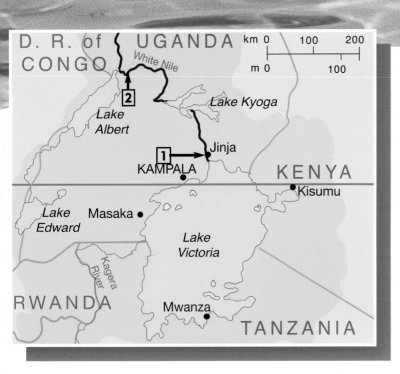

1.The source

The **source** is the start of a river. The Nile begins at Lake Victoria, Africa's biggest lake. Three countries, Kenya, Tanzania and Uganda, meet here. On the northern shore, water passes through a narrow opening, and the Nile is born. This place used to be a waterfall called the Ripon Falls, but a lake now covers the spot.

▼ **The Ripon Falls are now covered by a lake, which formed when a dam was built downstream. This tree marks the spot which was the source of the Nile.**

Finding the source

For years, the source of the Nile was a mystery to Europeans. In 1857, two British explorers, Richard Burton and John Hannington Speke, went in search of the source. They walked for months from the East African coast, and finally reached Lake Tanganyika. Burton thought this was the source, but Arab traders told them an even bigger lake lay upstream.

Burton was too ill to continue, but Speke carried on. In 1858 he reached a huge lake, which he named Lake Victoria after the British queen of the time. He claimed this lake was the source of the Nile, but Burton disagreed.

In 1860, Speke began another expedition to prove his theory. After two years of walking he reached a waterfall which he believed was the source of the Nile. He named it Ripon Falls. But Burton still disagreed. In 1875, an American journalist named Henry Stanley sailed right round Lake Victoria. He proved that Ripon Falls were the source of the Nile. Speke was right after all.

▲ **John Hannington Speke discovered the source of the Nile.**

The true source

Ripon Falls is the starting point of the Nile. But any of the streams that flow into Lake Victoria could claim to be the true source. The Kagera River, which begins in Burundi, is now thought to be the true source. Hundreds of streams tumble down the surrounding mountains into the lake. It is from here that the Nile is measured as the world's longest river.

Many uses

The Owens Falls Dam was built in 1954. An artificial lake called a **reservoir** built up behind the dam. The lake now covers Ripon Falls.

The dam is part of a power station. The flowing water turns giant wheels called turbines, which **generate** electricity. This type of energy is called **hydroelectric power** (HEP).

The dam lies in Uganda. In 2000, it was **extended** to meet Uganda's growing need for electricity. But Uganda still needs more energy. One answer is to build more dams, but the river has other uses too. Just below the Owens Falls Dam is a stretch of **rapids**, where the river crashes over large boulders. We board a rubber raft to descend the rapids. Hang on tight – this is one of the most exciting white-water rides in the world!

The Bujagli Falls

The Bujagli Falls MAP REF 1 are one of Uganda's top tourist attractions. Visitors come to see the foaming water, watch birds or shoot the rapids in a raft. But the Bujagli Falls are threatened by plans to build a new dam on the river here.

▼ **The Owens Falls Dam provides electricity for Uganda and its neighbour Kenya.**

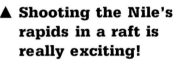

▲ Shooting the Nile's rapids in a raft is really exciting!

◄ Local children collect water from the Nile for drinking and washing.

For and against the dam

Local people do not agree about the dam. People who support the dam say it will double the amount of electricity the river produces. The building project will create new jobs. But some people are against the dam. They say it will destroy an important tourist attraction.

About 7,000 people will have to move as the land behind the dam floods. In 2005, the Ugandan government approved the plan, but four years later, building had still not begun.

▲ **Fishermen try to untangle water hyacinth from their nets.**

A pesky weed

We head downstream towards Lake Kyoga. We make our way through floating mats of a plant called water hyacinth. This plant looks pretty, but it can be a pest!

Water hyacinth grows very quickly. A patch of plant can double in size in just a week! Soon dense mats of water hyacinth cover the surface. They block sunlight and reduce the water's oxygen. This can kill fish. The weed makes it difficult to fish or travel the river by boat. It can even block the **turbines** at the Owen Falls Dam! Special dredging equipment can remove it. But the dredging work is dangerous because snakes and crocodiles lurk among the weeds.

In the 1990s, a type of beetle that eats water hyacinth was released into Lake Kyoga and other waterways. The beetles keep down the weed, but water hyacinth still chokes the surface in many places. Now people have come up with a new way of tackling water hyacinth. They plan to harvest it for animal feed.

The Basoga

The people who live along this stretch of the Nile are called the Basoga. There are many different peoples in Uganda. The Basoga are one of the biggest groups. They mainly work as farmers. A variety of crops, such as bananas, millet, beans and vegetables, grow well in the fertile soil. Most of the crops grown by the farmers are used to feed their families.

Coffee and sugar cane are grown for sale abroad.

There are more Basoga now than there used to be. The local population is increasing quickly. The increasing number of people means that good farmland is now scarce. The Basoga have started to catch fish to earn money and feed their families. The men and older boys do the fishing, in the Nile and local lakes. Women and girls help to clean, sort, dry and sell the fish.

▼ **Basoga women sort fish, which will then be dried. The fish will feed their families or be sold at market.**

◄ **Spray fills the air as the Nile plunges over Murchison Falls.**

Into the Rift Valley

We leave Lake Kyoga behind and head west. Soon the river drops over more rapids and waterfalls as it approaches the Great Rift Valley. This wide and incredibly long valley runs for 6,500 kilometres through East Africa. It formed as rocks shifted along giant cracks in the Earth's surface, called **faults**.

The rocks shifted because of pressure below ground. In some places, **lava** surged out of the cracks to create volcanoes. In other places, the land between the cracks slid down to form a wide valley floor.

Murchison Falls

The Nile enters the Rift Valley at Murchison Falls MAP REF 2, a spectacular waterfall. Here the river is forced through a narrow gap, which makes it flow faster. Then it plunges 40 metres to the valley floor.

The falls formed where water crosses from hard rock onto softer rock. The softer rock got worn away to form a sheer drop. Local people call it Bajao – 'devil's place'. The waterfall is

far too dangerous for us to paddle down. We leave the rubber raft and walk around the falls. We board another boat, this time a river launch, at the base.

National Park

Murchison Falls National Park is a popular tourist attraction. The river launch takes us to the foot of the falls. Here we are deafened by the roaring water and drenched by spray. The park lies in a poor part of Uganda. Tourism is an important money-earner here.

▲ **Hippos spend the day wallowing in the cool river. In the evening they come ashore to munch plants.**

The park is also famous for its wildlife. We see lions, elephants, giraffes and buffalo. Hippos swim in the river, and crocodiles lurk along the banks. Along much of the Nile, most crocodiles have been killed by local people. This is our best chance to see these scary reptiles. The very biggest crocs can measure six metres long and weigh 700 kilograms!

We continue by river launch as we head towards the country of Sudan.

2. The Upper Nile

Soon after Murchison Falls the Nile flows through a deep lake, Lake Albert. Then it heads into the Sudan. The river is now wider and slower, except for a stretch called Al-Jabal. Here it surges through narrow gorges and over rapids. We fly over this stretch and rejoin the river at Juba. Soon we reach a huge swamp called the Sudd.

▼ **Dinka men fish with spears. The fish come up to the surface at dusk.**

Dinka herders

Juba is the main city in southern Sudan. The Dinka people live in this region. They mainly live by breeding cattle. Cattle are very important to Dinka society. A person's wealth is measured in cattle. The cattle are rarely killed, but are used for milk and trading. Even their dung is burned as fuel. The smoke helps to keep off mosquitoes.

Dinka men and boys look after the cattle. Boys as young as eight years old lead their herds to water and fresh **grazing**. During the wet season there is plenty of lush pasture. During the dry

▲ **Dinka boys bring their cattle to the Nile to drink. The animals graze lush plants by the river.**

season they lead the cattle down to the Nile. Wild animals such as gazelle and wildebeest also head for the river. The Dinka hunt these for meat and hides. They also fish in the river.

Civil war

Unfortunately, this region has been badly hit by war. A **civil war** began here in 1955 and there has been fighting on and off ever since. Villages have been destroyed and people have died. Some grazing areas are now too dangerous to use.

▲ The Sudd is famous for birds. Here a fish eagle flies off with its prey in its claws.

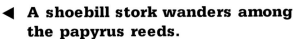

◀ A shoebill stork wanders among the papyrus reeds.

A huge swamp

North of Juba the land levels off. The Nile now flows through much flatter country. During the rainy season, the river spreads over the land to flood a huge area.

Marshland plants, such as **papyrus**, grow in thick clumps and block the flow of water. The river drains into an enormous swamp called the Sudd. The word Sudd means 'barrier'. This is one of the biggest wetlands in the world. It covers 130,000 square kilometres in the rainy season.

▶ **This digger carved the channel of the Jonglei Canal.**

The Sudd helps to control the flow of the Nile. In the rainy season it acts like a giant sponge, soaking up excess water. It slowly releases the water in the dry season. However, about half of all the water is lost, as it sinks into the soil or **evaporates** (rises) into the air.

The Jonglei Canal

The people of Sudan and Egypt have a growing need for water. In the 1970s, the two countries made a plan to use the water which was normally lost in the Sudd. Engineers designed a 360-kilometre canal that would bypass the swamp MAP REF 1. The canal would provide water for farming. It would also make a shortcut on the journey along the Nile.

Digging began in 1978. A huge digger called a bucketwheel carved out the **channel**. But work stopped in 1983, due to the war in Sudan. Two-thirds of the **canal** had been dug, but now it may never be finished. In fact, that may not be a bad thing, because the canal would have disturbed the Dinka herders and their way of life. Local wildlife would have suffered too.

We continue by canoe through the channels of the Sudd.

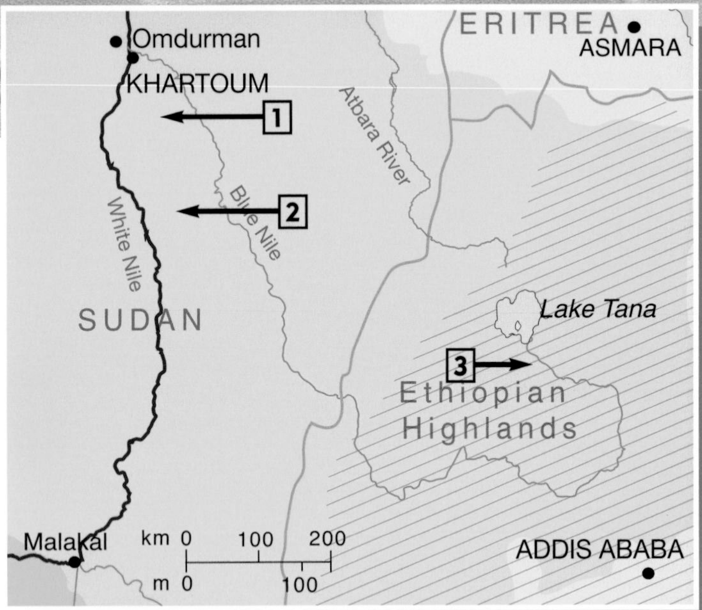

Omdurman
KHARTOUM
ERITREA
ASMARA
Atbara River
1
2
Blue Nile
White Nile
SUDAN
Lake Tana
3
Ethiopian Highlands
Malakal
km 0 100 200
m 0 100
ADDIS ABABA

3. Where rivers join

North of the Sudd several rivers join the Nile. A river that joins another one is called a **tributary**. The Sobat joins the Nile near the town of Malakal. About 500 kilometres downstream, the Blue Nile joins the White Nile. The rivers meet near the twin cities of Khartoum and Omdurman. From now on the river is simply called the Nile.

▼ **These workers are harvesting cotton by hand. Cotton is an important crop.**

▲ **Farmers water their fields using irrigation channels.**

Irrigation

The triangle of land between the White Nile and the Blue Nile is called Al-Jazirah. This region is very dry. It receives less than 25 centimetres of rain a year. Farmers have to divert river water to wet their fields. This is called irrigation.

In 1925 a major irrigation project started here. It was called the Gezira Project MAP REF 1 . Water from the Blue Nile was channelled to the fields. The Gezira Project still exists, but it now covers a much bigger area – about a million hectares.

We pass farmers harvesting cotton. This is a cash crop - a crop grown for sale abroad. Sugar cane is also grown. The cane is processed in a large factory at Kenana MAP REF 2 .

Salty soil

Some of the fields we pass have a whitish surface. This is caused by salts and minerals left in the soil when water evaporates in the hot sun. The salts build up on irrigated land. This problem is called **salinisation** and the Gezira Project has made it worse.

Salts build up when too much water is used in irrigation. Instead of being absorbed by plants, the water sits on the surface. Then it evaporates – rises into the air as a gas, leaving the salt behind. Salinisation is a problem for farmers because plants will not grow in salty soil.

The Blue Nile

North of Al-Jazirah the Blue Nile joins the White Nile. The Blue Nile is an important river in its own right. It provides over 60 per cent of the Nile's water – so it is really the White Nile's big brother.

We take a side trip from our main route. We board a small plane, and fly over the Blue Nile from its source to where it joins the White Nile. The Blue Nile starts off as a small stream called the Abay. It flows from a spring in the highlands of Ethiopia.

▲ **The Blue Nile carved this beautiful gorge in Ethiopia.**

The people of the region believe the spring is holy and can heal the sick. The main religion here is the Ethiopian Orthodox Church. Pilgrims travel a long way to visit the sacred waters.

An amazing waterfall

The Blue Nile flows into Lake Tana. Beyond the lake it plunges over a dramatic waterfall called Tis Abay Falls MAP REF 3 . As our plane skims low over the falls we see spray

▲ The Blue Nile drops 45 metres
at the Tis Abay Falls.

rising like smoke. Tis Abay means
'smoke of the Nile'.

Grand Canyon of Africa

After the falls the Blue Nile surges
through a deep gorge. The sheer walls
are 1,000 metres high in places. The
churning water has cut deep into the
rock. Some people call this the Grand
Canyon of Africa.

Damming the Blue Nile

In the past, Ethiopia used little of the
Nile water. But now there are more
people, and a growing need for water.

The Ethiopian government has
built over 200 small dams along
the Blue Nile. During the 1990s
there were plans to build a much
larger dam near Lake Tana. This
would have greatly reduced the
water flowing downstream.

Further downriver, there would
have been less water for Sudan and
Egypt. This could have caused a lot
of trouble. Luckily in 1999, the
countries along the Nile made an
agreement about sharing river water.
This has helped to keep the peace.

Waters meet

Back at Khartoum, we can see where the Blue Nile meets the White Nile. A place where two rivers meet is called a **confluence**.

The two rivers are very different. The White Nile has an almost constant flow. This is due to the Sudd, which soaks up excess water and then releases it slowly. In contrast, the Blue Nile floods during the rainy season between July and October.

By the time it reaches Khartoum, the Blue Nile is often three metres higher than usual. In 1998 it rose by 16 metres, causing a destructive flood. The surging waters of the Blue Nile actually hold back the weaker White Nile. The waters of White Nile spread out to form a temporary lake. This can cause flooding.

The twin cities

The twin cities of Khartoum and Omdurman lie at the confluence of the White Nile and the Blue Nile.

▼ **The Blue Nile joins the wider White Nile. In the rainy season the Blue Nile holds back the White Nile, which then becomes much wider, as you can see here.**

Like the rivers, they are very different. Khartoum, the capital of Sudan, is a busy city with many modern buildings. Omdurman across the river is older and more traditional.

Whirling Dervishes

We visit the souk, or market, in Omdurman. There we see traders bargaining as they have done for centuries. Next we visit a mosque. On a Friday evening Sufi Muslims spin around here as they dance and chant prayers. They believe spinning brings them closer to God. They are called Whirling Dervishes. This amazing

▲ A cloth store at the souk in Omdurman.

sight reminds us that from now on, the people we meet will be Muslim.

The slave trade

The word Khartoum means 'elephant's trunk'. The name refers to the shape of the land where the rivers join. You can see the elephant's trunk in the photo on the opposite page. Khartoum was once a centre for the slave trade. Traders captured slaves from southern Sudan. The slaves were sold to the Egyptian army. The slave trade continued here until it was banned around 1870.

◄ A Whirling Dervish spins as he prays.

We catch a ride on a barge and head towards the Nile cataracts.

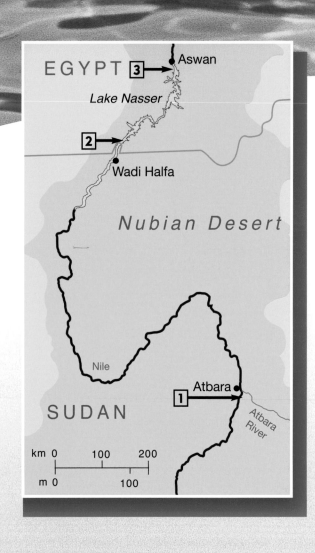

EGYPT **3** → Aswan

Lake Nasser

2 →

Wadi Halfa

Nubian Desert

Nile

1 → Atbara

Atbara River

SUDAN

km 0   100   200

m 0   100

4. The Nile cataracts

We leave the lush swamps of Sudan behind and enter a region that is mostly desert. The river is mainly calm here, but then it surges over a series of rapids. The rapids are called **cataracts** and there are five of them. We have to go around by land as the water is too rough to sail by barge.

▼ **As the Nile passes through the desert it creates a strip of fertile land about 25 kilometres wide.**

Ancient Nubia

As we continue north we begin to pass some of the ancient **monuments** that have made the Nile famous. About 2,700 years ago this region was ruled by a people called the Nubians. They were an advanced civilisation like the Egyptians.

The capital of the Nubian kingdom was Meroë MAP REF 1. There are many pyramids here, but they are smaller than the ones we will see in Egypt. We admire a temple, which is decorated with carved elephants. The Nubians sold elephants to the Egyptians, who used them in battle.

▲ **Pyramids at Meroë. Meroë was the capital of ancient Nubia.**

The people of Meroë were skilled metal-workers. They used water wheels to irrigate their land. But we don't know a lot about them because no one can read their writing.

The Atbara

At the town of Atbara another great river joins the Nile. The Atbara River begins in the Ethiopian Highlands. It floods in the rainy season like the Blue Nile. The Atbara is sometimes called the Nile's little brother. It provides about 15 per cent of the Nile's water. But in the dry season it contains little water.

The Nubians today

No one knows why the ancient Nubians became less powerful. Today, modern Nubians still live in northern Sudan and southern Egypt.

In 1960, the **construction** of the Aswan High Dam in Egypt affected the Nubians. The dam partly blocked the river's flow. Water built up behind the dam to form a huge lake, Lake Nasser. The valley behind the dam was flooded. About 90,000 Nubians who lived there had to move. Ancient towns and also modern ones were flooded.

Nubians still live close to the Nile. They wear long flowing clothes, which feel cool in the hot desert sun. The women wear dresses, colourful headgear and lots of jewellery. The men wear a white ankle-length robe called the galabia. Perhaps we should wear Nubian clothes as we continue our journey, as it is getting very hot!

Desert wildlife

Camels are probably the most famous desert animal. They can cope with scorching heat and go for several days without water. The Nubians and other local people use camels to transport goods across the desert. Camels are known as 'ships of the desert'. A thirsty camel can drink 100 litres of water in just ten minutes! We take a camel ride into the desert to spot wildlife.

▼ **A Nubian boat-builder wears traditional robes. You can also see boats at various stages of being built.**

▲ **A thirsty camel and a donkey drink from a water trough.**

▶ **The fennec fox hides in its burrow during the hottest time of day.**

Desert animals include the fennec fox. This little fox has huge ears that give off heat like miniature radiators. This helps the fox to keep cool. The fox also uses its ears to pinpoint prey. Like many desert creatures, the fennec fox is active at night. It rests in its burrow by day and comes out to hunt at dusk. During the day few creatures are active, but we see some lizards and beetles scuttling over the sand.

The cataracts

The Nile cataracts formed where a band of hard rocks crosses the river. The softer rocks just downstream have worn away to create a sudden drop. Boats cannot cross the rapids. However the six cataracts are now five, because one has been flooded by Lake Nasser.

▲ The temple of Abu Simbel was saved from the rising waters of Lake Nasser.

We sail across the lake, which is enormous. It's hard to imagine that this was once desert land. The lake dates from the building of the Aswan High Dam.

Aswan High Dam

For centuries, the Nile flooded each year to spread rich **silt** over the land. This allowed Egyptian farmers to grow crops. But the floods were unpredictable. They could be slight, or last for months on end. As Egypt's **population** grew, the uncertainty made it hard to grow enough food.

In the late 1800s, Egypt decided to control the Nile's flow by building a dam. The first dam was finished in 1902, but it was too small to control the floods. In 1960, work began on a bigger dam. It took 50,000 workers eleven years to build.

The Aswan High Dam succeeded in controlling the floods. It provides farmers downstream with a regular supply of water. It has increased the region's farmland. It also generates electricity. However, it has created some problems, as we will see later on.

Abu Simbel

The magnificent temple of Abu Simbel stands near Lake Nasser MAP REF 2. It was built by a great Egyptian pharaoh called Ramses II. It is about

▲ These workers are building the power plant at the Aswan High Dam in the 1960s.

3,000 years old – but has not always stood on its present **site**!

In the 1960s the temple was threatened by water as Lake Nasser formed behind the Aswan Dam. Luckily, Egypt launched a rescue mission, helped by money from many other countries. The temple was taken apart block by block, and rebuilt on higher ground.

◀ Date palms grow on fertile land by the Nile.

We leave our boat near the Aswan High Dam to visit Aswan town by camel. Hang on tight!

5. The Nile valley

Around 2,500 years ago, the Greek writer Herodotus said: 'Egypt is the gift of the Nile'. He meant that the Egyptian civilisation depended on the river for its food and farming. As we enter the Nile Valley we see this is still true today. Nearly all Egyptians live along the narrow strip of fertile land by the river, or in the Nile Delta where our journey will end.

Aswan

The name Aswan comes from an ancient word meaning trade. Trade is still important in Aswan, which has a busy market. It lies at the furthest point that can be reached by boat from the Mediterranean. It is also the last city on the railway from Cairo.

The Aswan High Dam dominates the town. This massive dam has a power station. River water turns turbines, which generate electricity. The dam produces about 15 per cent of Egypt's electricity.

◀ **Feluccas drift on the Nile near Aswan.**

▼ **Colourful spices on sale at Aswan market.**

The power has helped Aswan's industries develop. Fertiliser is one of the main products made here.

Elephantine Island

We board a sailing boat called a felucca and head towards Cairo. These little boats with triangular sails have cruised the Nile for hundreds of years. Soon we catch sight of a rocky outcrop in the middle of the river – Elephantine Island.

Some people believe Elephantine Island is so-called because it looks like a group of elephants bathing. Other people think that ivory was once traded here. This is one of the few places where a rocky island splits the Nile into two channels.

Tourism

Tourism is very important to Egypt. The Nile is one of the main attractions. It is popular with visitors mostly because of all the ancient buildings along its banks. Tourists travel the Nile by felucca or take a luxury cruise boat.

Tourism is one of Egypt's top money-earners. In fact it is the second-biggest earner after oil, which is mined here. Some tourists travel independently and use local services.

But many people take an organised tour by cruise boat. Many of the cruise boats are owned by big companies. They have everything on board, not only food and cabins to sleep in, but also guides and souvenirs. This means that local restaurants, hotels, guides and souvenir shops don't earn very much money.

▼ ▶ **Most tourists take a cruise boat. But a trip on a felucca gives a real sense of the river.**

The temple of Horus

The temple of Horus, the falcon god, at Edfu, is one of the most famous sights in the Nile Valley. It is over 2,000 years old, but very well preserved. This is because it had been mostly covered by sand for centuries until it was discovered in 1860.

In ancient times, Edfu was famous for its quarries. It was one of the main sources of **sandstone** rock along the Nile. Sandstone is good for carving. The temple of Horus is covered with amazing carvings. It took 180 years to build. The carvings were once brightly painted, but now most of the paint has worn off.

Quarrying on the Nile

Huge blocks of sandstone from Edfu and also Aswan were carried down the Nile by barge. The huge temples at Luxor and Karnak downstream were built with stone from Edfu. The huge stones could not have been transported without the river. The great temples might never have been built.

▶ **A guide waits for tourists at the temple of Horus. The statue is of Horus, the falcon god.**

'Fellahin' farmers

As we sail towards Luxor we see farmers working in the fields beside the river. The farmers are called 'fellahin'. They mostly grow food for their families. Any extra is sold at market. Some farmers grow sugar or cotton to sell.

The farming methods here are often basic. Oxen and buffalo are still used to pull ploughs as well as tractors. Farmers draw water from the Nile using a simple machine called a **shaduf**. This is a long pole with a

▲ **A farmer draws water from the Nile using a shaduf.**

weight at one end and a bucket at the other. The bucket is lowered into the water and then lifted again using the weight. The shaduf has been used in Egypt for over 2,000 years.

Sights of Luxor

We dock at Luxor and go ashore to explore this incredibly ancient city. There are several magnificent temples in the town and by the river. There are as many tourists here as local people!

Valley of the Kings

The famous Valley of the Kings lies on the opposite bank MAP REF 1. This hot, dusty valley is full of tombs. Here Egyptian kings and queens were buried with their treasure and possessions. Almost all of the tombs were raided centuries ago, and so are now empty. But in 1922 an **archaeologist**, named Howard Carter, discovered the lost tomb of the king Tutankhamun. It was packed with golden treasure.

The most famous treasure was Tutankhamun's funeral mask, made of solid gold. It is now in the museum in Cairo. We visit Tutankhamun's tomb. Some people once believed that anyone who entered the tomb would be cursed. Enter if you dare!

▼ **Fields of sugar cane grow by the river. In the distance you can see a temple and the way to the Valley of the Kings.**

Giant statues

On our way back to Luxor we pass two giant statues called the Colossi of Memnon. These huge seated figures were once part of another temple. Now they look very odd, surrounded by fields of sugar cane.

Cash crops

As we head on towards Cairo we pass more fields of sugar cane. This is one of the main crops grown for sale in Egypt. Crops grown mainly for sale are called cash crops. The cut cane is loaded on carts pulled by donkeys or tractors. It goes to the railway station, then on to factories that process the cane to make sugar.

Egypt's production of sugar cane more than doubled between 1970 and 2000. But growing cash crops like this can cause problems. It means there is less good land to grow food for Egypt's people. Also, Egyptian farmers suffer if the price of sugar drops.

A useful reed

We notice papyrus growing by the river. This tall reed once grew all along the Nile. It was very useful to the ancient Egyptians. The stems were used to make ropes, mats and boats. The roots were eaten as food, burned as fuel

▼ **Children help to gather cut sugar cane, which will be loaded onto railway trucks.**

▲ **A craft worker lays strips of papyrus crosswise to make paper.**

and even used to make perfume. But the most important use of papyrus was to make paper.

People made paper by slicing papyrus stems into long, thin strips. The strips were soaked in water, then laid crosswise. When a weight was put on top, the strips stuck together with sap. The sheets were dried and then rubbed with shells or ivory. This made a smooth writing surface. Papyrus is still made today. The reed is grown in special plantations. Paintings on papyrus paper are sold to tourists.

Busy banks

As we approach the city of Cairo, we are entering the most densely populated part of Egypt. But the large numbers of people cause **pollution** along the river. Litter, sewage, chemicals from farming and factories, and soap from washing all add to the pollution.

▼ **When people wash their clothes in the Nile, soap enters the river. This causes pollution.**

The Pyramids of Giza

Before we enter Cairo we take a side trip to see the famous Pyramids of Giza MAP REF 2. Many people think these are the greatest wonder of the world. The pyramids are gigantic tombs made from huge stone blocks. The Great Pyramid contains over two million limestone blocks! It took 20 years to build and stands 147 metres tall.

People used to think the pyramids were built by slaves. But now experts believe that they were mostly built by farmers. During the Nile's annual flood, farmers could not work in the fields. They worked on the pyramids instead, in return for food and shelter.

We stand before these enormous structures and try to imagine all the effort that went into building them. The task would have been quite impossible without the Nile to transport stone.

◀ **The famous statue of the Sphinx guards the Great Pyramid of Giza.**

▼ **The view from the top of the Cairo Tower.**

▲ **A crowded ferry on the Nile can be a quicker way to travel around Cairo than to go by car.**

Crowded Cairo

We enter the huge, bustling city of Cairo. This vast city is a mixture of old and new. There are modern skyscrapers and shopping malls. Just a short distance away are markets and narrow streets that have not changed much in 500 years.

Cairo is one of the world's biggest cities. Around 16 million people live here. One of the best ways to see the city is from the top of the Cairo Tower. This 187-metre tower stands on an island in the Nile.

Back at ground level we notice people living on boats moored along the banks.

Cairo has a shortage of housing. Some people even live in ancient tombs, in a district called the City of the Dead!

Air pollution

Air pollution is a serious problem in Cairo. It can make it hard to breathe. The pollution is mainly caused by all the cars and trucks that fill the streets. During rush hours the streets are incredibly crowded. The noise of honking car horns is deafening! We have to be very careful as we cross the street.

We board a small motor boat for the last stage of our journey to the delta.

MEDITERRANEAN SEA

Rosetta
Damietta
Port Said
Alexandria
1
CAIRO
Suez
EGYPT
Nile
km 0   50   100
m 0   50
RED
SEA

6.The Nile delta

About 20 kilometres north of Cairo
the Nile divides into two main
branches. These are the Rosetta
and Damietta Rivers. The enormous
triangle of land between the rivers is
the Nile Delta. This land is very
fertile and covered with farmland.
As a result the delta is densely
populated. We explore the region
on our way to the sea.

▼ **The image taken by satellite shows
the fan-shape of the Nile Delta. The
red shows the water.**

Delta farming

The Nile Delta has been an important farming region since ancient times. It is often called 'the bread basket of Egypt because it provides so much food. In the rainy season, the annual floods spread a rich layer of fertile silt over this area. But since the Aswan High Dam was built, the river no longer floods. Farmers have to put artificial fertiliser on their crops instead.

Flood control meant that new areas could be farmed. Egypt's farmlands increased by a third after the Aswan High Dam was built. Most of the new land was in the delta. Cotton and rice are the main crops grown here. Wheat, citrus, vegetables and date palms are also grown.

Greening the desert

In the 1990s, Egypt began a major new building project in this region. The Al Salam canal and pipeline will divert water from the Nile to irrigate the desert east of the delta. If the plan works, the desert here will become green and fertile. People could move to this new farming area from the Nile Valley, which is overcrowded.

▲ **You need a good head for heights to harvest dates!**

▼ **Part of the Al Salam pipeline, which will carry Nile water to the desert.**

Effects of the Dam

We are now more than 1,000 kilometres from the Aswan High Dam. But the dam has greatly affected this region. Each year, the river added fertile silt to the delta. Now this no longer happens the delta is shrinking. It is being **eroded** (worn away) both by the river and by waves on the coast.

Without river silt, farmers use a lot of fertiliser on their fields. When this drains into the river it causes pollution.

Fewer fish

Fish were once abundant in coastal waters. They fed on minerals washed out to sea by the river. The coasts around the river mouth were rich fishing grounds. But the number of fish caught fell dramatically once the dam was built. This was because there were less food for the fish.

The effects of the Aswan High Dam has taught planners to think very carefully when anyone suggests building a new dam.

▲ **Fishermen's nets are often empty since the Aswan Dam was built.**

Ports and canals

Much of Egypt's industry is located in the delta. Trade and shipping are also important. The coastal city of Alexandria has many factories. It is also Egypt's main port, and handles 80 per cent of the country's trade.

A canal links Alexandria to the River Nile. This allows cargo and passenger boats to travel inland as far as Aswan.

On the eastern side of the delta, Port Said is another major port. It lies at the entrance to the Suez Canal

MAP REF 1 , which links the Mediterranean to the Red Sea. This canal was opened in 1869.

The Suez Canal provides a shortcut for ships sailing between the Atlantic and the Indian Ocean. Without it, ships would have to sail right round the tip of Africa. Ships pay a fee to use the canal. This is a very important money-earner for Egypt.

▼ **The Suez Canal links the Mediterranean with the Indian Ocean. It is 193 kilometres long.**

Looking to the future

In 2000, there about 160 million people living in the Nile **basin**. Nearly twice that number live in all the countries that border the Nile. These countries have some of the fastest-growing populations in the world. Both Egypt and Sudan depend on the Nile for water. The number of people is rising fast in both these countries. This will increase the demand for river water.

Changing climate

The Earth's **climate** is getting warmer. This is called global warming. Scientists believe this is happening because air pollution from factories, cars and power stations is trapping heat near Earth's surface. In future, **global warming** is likely to affect the Nile region, like many other areas worldwide. Global warming is also making the weather more extreme and less predictable. Droughts and floods are becoming more common.

Global warming is starting to melt the ice in the polar regions. If this continues, the melting ice will make sea levels rise. Experts think sea levels could rise by as much as one metre by 2100. If this happens, up to a third of the Nile Delta could be under sea water.

▶ **Fishermen cast their nets in the delta. Fishing could become even more important in future – especially if part of the delta floods.**

Journey's End

Our journey ends where the Nile meets the Mediterranean Sea. We have travelled more than 6,600 kilometres along the longest river in the world.

The Nile continues to fascinate people. The river has given up some of its secrets. But there is still a lot we don't know about the past – or the future – of the Nile.

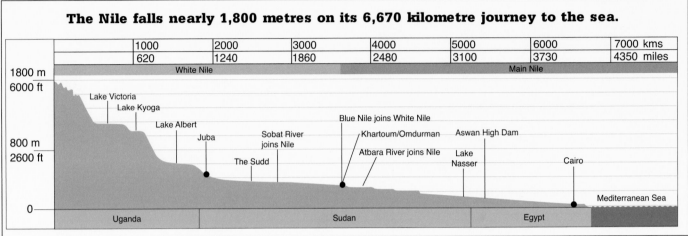

The Nile falls nearly 1,800 metres on its 6,670 kilometre journey to the sea.

		1000	2000	3000	4000	5000	6000	7000 kms
		620	1240	1860	2480	3100	3730	4350 miles

White Nile · Main Nile

1800 m / 6000 ft
800 m / 2600 ft
0

Lake Victoria
Lake Kyoga
Lake Albert
Juba
The Sudd
Sobat River joins Nile
Blue Nile joins White Nile
Khartoum/Omdurman
Atbara River joins Nile
Aswan High Dam
Lake Nasser
Cairo
Mediterranean Sea

Uganda · Sudan · Egypt

Further information

Useful websites

http://touregypt.net/wildegypt/
Includes lots of information about the wildlife and national parks along the Nile in Egypt.

http://library.thinkquest.org/16645/the_land/nile_river.shtml
This website has information about the Nile, with facts on climate, flooding, dams and irrigation. It describes the people living along the river.

http://www.factmonster.com/ce6/world/A0835683.html
A website with facts and figures about the Nile, including the history of the region, farming and also shipping on the Nile.

http://www.utdallas.edu/geosciences/remsens/Nile
Information about the Nile and its tributaries and lakes. This site has facts on irrigation and local rocks, and also maps of the region.

Books

Changing Face of Egypt by Ron Ragsdale (Wayland, 2007)

Geography Detective: Rivers by Jen Green (Wayland, 2006)

Geography Now: Rivers around the World by Jen Green (Wayland, 2008)

Picture the Past: The Nile by Jane Shuter (Heinemann, 2005)

Glossary

archaeologist a scientist who studies the remains of past civilizations.

basin the total area drained by a river and its tributaries.

canal an artificial waterway.

cash crops crops that are grown for sale.

cataract another word for rapids.

channel the passage through which a river flows.

civil war a war between people of the same country.

climate the long-term weather patterns of a region.

confluence a place where rivers meet.

construction when something is built.

dam a barrier that diverts or holds back water.

delta a flat, swampy area of land that forms as a river drops silt at its mouth.

dhow a small sailing boat with triangular sails.

divert to change the direction of something.

drought long periods without rain.

erode when rocks and soil are worn away by rain, wind or ice.

evaporate when water rises into the air in the form of a gas called water vapour.

extend to make something bigger or longer.

fault a deep crack in the rocks at Earth's surface.

generate to make electricity.

global warming warming temperatures worldwide, caused by air pollution.

gorge a deep, narrow valley with sheer sides.

grazing when animals such as deer or cattle graze, or eat grass.

hydroelectricity electricity that is made using energy from fast-flowing water.

irrigation when farmers water their fields using water channelled from a river.

lava hot, melted rock from deep below Earth's surface that erupts from a volcano.

monument a building or statue made in memory of a person or an event.

papyrus a type of reed that grows by the Nile.

pollution when the air, water or soil is harmed by a material that doesn't belong there.

population the number of people living in an area.

rapids an area of white water where a river crashes over rocks.

reservoir an artificial lake used to store water, made by damming a river or stream.

salinisation when salt builds up in the soil.

sandstone a type of rock.

shaduf a machine used to raise water.

silt fine sand or mud carried along by a river.

site a place.

souk a word for a market.

source the place where a river begins.

tributary a minor river or stream that joins the main river.

turbine a machine powered by steam or water that is used to produce electricity.

Index

Journey Along a River

Contents of titles in the series:

WAYLAND